Blah Blah Blah

A play with songs

Brian Marshall

Samuel French—London
New York-Toronto-Hollywood

Copyright © 1998 by Samuel French Ltd
All Rights Reserved

BLAH BLAH BLAH is fully protected under the copyright laws of the British Commonwealth, including Canada, the United States of America, and all other countries of the Copyright Union. All rights, including professional and amateur stage productions, recitation, lecturing, public reading, motion picture, radio broadcasting, television and the rights of translation into foreign languages are strictly reserved.

ISBN 978-0-573-15210-8

www.samuelfrench.co.uk
www.samuelfrench.com

FOR AMATEUR PRODUCTION ENQUIRIES

UNITED KINGDOM AND WORLD EXCLUDING NORTH AMERICA

plays@samuelfrench.co.uk

020 7255 4302/01

Each title is subject to availability from Samuel French, depending upon country of performance.

CAUTION: Professional and amateur producers are hereby warned that BLAH BLAH BLAH is subject to a licensing fee. Publication of this play does not imply availability for performance. Both amateurs and professionals considering a production are strongly advised to apply to the appropriate agent before starting rehearsals, advertising, or booking a theatre. A licensing fee must be paid whether the title is presented for charity or gain and whether or not admission is charged.

The professional rights in this play are controlled by Samuel French Ltd, 24-32 Stephenson Way, London, NW1 2HD.

No one shall make any changes in this title for the purpose of production. No part of this book may be reproduced, stored in a retrieval system, or transmitted in any form, by any means, now known or yet to be invented, including mechanical, electronic, photocopying, recording, videotaping, or otherwise, without the prior written permission of the publisher. No one shall upload this title, or part of this title, to any social media websites.

The right of Brian Marshall to be identified as author of this work has been asserted in accordance with Section 77 of the Copyright, Designs and Patents Act 1988.

CHARACTERS

Id
Voice
Chorus play all other roles:

Kid	**Old Fart**
Mum	**Son**
Dad	**Daughter**
Teacher	**Nurse**
New Kid	**Children**
Death	**Schoolkids**
Yoof	**Teenagers**
Boss	**Workers**
Secretary	**Clubbers**
Dealer	**Cheerleaders**
Passion	**Muddlers**
Middle Age	**Patients**
Men-In-White-Coats	**Party-Goers**
Shrink	**Geriatrics**

COPYRIGHT INFORMATION
(See also page ii)

This play is fully protected under the Copyright Laws of the British Commonwealth of Nations, the United States of America and all countries of the Berne and Universal Copyright Conventions.

All rights, including Stage, Motion Picture, Radio, Television, Public Reading, and Translation into Foreign Languages, are strictly reserved.

No part of this publication may lawfully be reproduced in ANY form or by any means — photocopying, typescript, recording (including video-recording), manuscript, electronic, mechanical, or otherwise — or be transmitted or stored in a retrieval system, without prior permission.

Licences are issued subject to the understanding that it shall be made clear in all advertising matter that the audience will witness an amateur performance; that the names of the authors of the plays shall be included on all announcements and on all programmes; and that the integrity of the authors' work will be preserved.

The Royalty Fee is subject to contract and subject to variation at the sole discretion of Samuel French Ltd.

In Theatres or Halls seating Four Hundred or more the fee will be subject to negotiation.

In Territories Overseas the fee quoted in this Acting Edition may not apply. A fee will be quoted on application to our local authorized agent, or if there is no such agent, on application to Samuel French Ltd, London.

VIDEO-RECORDING OF AMATEUR PRODUCTIONS

Please note that the copyright laws governing video-recording are extremely complex and that it should not be assumed that any play may be video-recorded for *whatever purpose* without first obtaining the permission of the appropriate agents. The fact that a play is published by Samuel French Ltd does not indicate that video rights are available or that Samuel French Ltd controls such rights.

"And when I beheld my devil I found him serious, thorough, profound, solemn; it was the Spirit of Gravity, through him all things are ruined. One does not kill by anger but by laughter. Come let us kill the Spirit of Gravity."

Nietzsche

"Blah, blah, blah…"

Anon.

PRODUCTION NOTES

Set: A bare stage with, perhaps, a scaffolding structure or rostra upstage to create various areas for the action.

Props: Most sequences are mimed with no use of actual props.

Costume: Uniform and androgynous, such as black leotards and T-shirts over which bits of costume (e.g. hats and jackets) can be added to create character. White half-face masks should be worn throughout.

Actors: All parts except Mum, Dad, Teacher, and Men-In-White-Coats can be played by actors of either sex, but in the interests of brevity the masculine personal pronoun is used wherever gender is not obvious.

MUSIC

Music for the songs by Brian Marshall is available on hire from Samuel French Ltd

A licence issued by Samuel French Ltd to perform this play only includes permission to use the songs by Brian Marshall specified in this copy. If any other music is used in conjunction with this play permission must be sought as under:

Where the place of performance is already licensed by the Performing Right Society a return of the music used must be made to them. If the place of performance is not so licensed then application should be made to the Performing Right Society, 29 Berners Street, London, W1.

A separate and additional licence from Phonographic Performances Ltd, 1 Upper James Street, London, W1R 3HG is needed whenever commercial recordings are used.

If Brian Marshall's songs are used out of context of the play a return must be made to the Performing Right Society.

Backing tapes - vocal and non-vocal - are available from the author. Please apply to Brian Marshall c/o The Editorial Department, Samuel French Ltd, 52 Fitzroy Street, London W1P 6JR.

For my father, Stanley

BLAH BLAH BLAH

Everywhere and nowhere

The house Lights dim to darkness and we hear an orchestra tuning up. The opening chord of Pink Floyd's Shine On You Crazy Diamond *is heard; a long, ominous drone. The Lights fade up very slowly with the music*

Through a carpet of smoke we see Chorus standing with their backs to the audience. Motionless, they appear like ghostly silhouettes. Chorus turn around one by one and enact a small mime or gesture indicating a state or emotion, e.g. anger, seduction, frustration, innocence; then freeze. Only Id, C, *remains with his back to the audience. Chorus stare at the audience for some time. The silence becomes excruciating, embarrassing, until it is broken by a Voice from amongst the audience*

Voice Well, well—what have we here? "Theatre" with a capital T no doubt. Come on then, we haven't got all night.

Id turns around and produces a scroll

Id (*clearing his throat*) Ladies and gentlemen...
Voice A prologue, no less.
Id What *you* are about to see is... (*After a pensive pause*) No. What you are *about* to see is... No! No! What you are about to see *is*... (*He stares vacantly at the audience*)
Voice I do believe the poor dear has dried.

One of the Chorus (Chorus 1) approaches Id and smiles as if about to whisper. Suddenly Chorus 1 knees Id in the crotch, accompanied by a crash on drums. Chorus break into hysterical laughter then just as suddenly stop. Chorus 1 bows and returns to the line

Id (*clearing his throat*) Ladies and gentlemen, what you are about to see is... (*He consults the scroll—it is blank*) What you are about to see.

Chorus break into applause, then suddenly stop

Voice Oh, it's one of those plays. Contrived absurdity. The nonsensical posing as the profound. Very well then, do your worst.

Id mounts a soapbox to the side of the stage. Chorus become small Children and crawl around the floor

Id Ladies and gentlemen when we are (*he mimes quotation marks*) "children", we are told what is right and what is wrong. What is...
Child 1 Good and evil.
Child 2 Black and white.
Child 3 Truth and lies.
Child 4 Love and hate.
Id Heaven and... Heaven and... (*He stares vacantly at the audience*)
Voice Hell?
Id Exactly! Ladies and gentlemen, there is a certain sublime comfort to be had in trusting these Universal Truths.
Voice Ah! At last we're getting somewhere. Universal Truths. Good.

Chorus form a human pyramid. Kid looks on

Id Without hesitation we follow our elders, our parents and teachers, our government, our TV personalities, assured in the belief that they too live their lives by the same incontrovertible code of moral conduct that they bully into us on a daily basis.
Voice Come on then, what's your point?

Blah Blah Blah 3

Id Ladies and gentlemen, do you remember your surprise when...

There is a drum roll. Kid climbs up to crown the human pyramid

Kid Look, Ma! Top of the world!

At the moment of triumph, the pyramid collapses accompanied by a crash on the drums

Voice Was that supposed to be symbolic of something? Some supreme irony, perhaps? Never mind, there's nothing like a good sight gag to pick up a flagging script.
Id It is a well documented "fact" that most of our childhood is spent in a constant state of...
Child 1 Confusion!
Child 2 Anxiety!
Child 3 Alienation!
Id Spent in a fruitless search for...
Child 4 Approval!
Child 5 Unconditional love!
Child 6 Gratification!
Id To summarise, then...
Children I want my Mummy!
Id Ladies and gentlemen, an illustration.

Heavy traffic effect. In a pool of Light C, Mum, Dad and Kid mime travelling in a car. Mum and Dad are in front, Kid in the back. Chorus look on

Kid I am seven years old. This is my Mummy. And this is my Daddy. We are going to the seaside. I've never been to the seaside. The seaside is a long way. Mummy?
Mum (*angrily*) What?
Kid When will we get to the seaside?
Mum I don't know. Ask your father.
Kid Daddy?
Dad (*angrily*) What?

Kid When will we get to the seaside?
Dad I don't know, now shut up!
Mum (*shouting*) Don't shout at the kid!
Dad (*shouting*) Don't shout at me!
Kid Please don't fight.
Mum⎫
Dad ⎭ (*together*) Shut up!

The seaside. Effect of waves crashing and holiday makers making merry

The family mime getting out of the car, unpacking mountains of paraphernalia and hustling to the beach. Finding a good spot, Dad and Mum mark out their territory like wild animals. Settling, Dad opens a beer and guzzles it down whilst Mum gorges herself on the picnic food. Kid looks out at the sea and the sky with wide-eyed wonder

Kid Mummy?
Mum What?
Kid Who made the sky?
Mum I don't know. Ask your father.
Kid Daddy?
Dad What?
Kid Who made the sky?
Dad I don't know, now shut up!
Mum Don't shout at the kid!
Dad Don't shout at me!
Kid Please don't fight.
Dad ⎫
Mum⎭ (*together*) Shut up!
Dad Time you learned a thing or two!
Mum Time you stopped acting the fool!
Id Time for school! (*He rings a bell*)

Schoolroom

Chorus become Schoolkids and sit at the feet of the Teacher dutifully

Teacher Gather round little ones. Today we have someone new joining the class.
Schoolkids Oooo!

Mum and Dad pull a struggling Kid to the Teacher

Kid No, no, no…
Dad Yes.
Mum Yes.
Teacher (*grabbing Kid*) Yes. Tell the class your name, child.
Kid (*stuttering*) I d-d-don't kn-kn-know.

Schoolkids snigger and point at Kid

Teacher Stupid child! Now pay attention, little ones.
Blah blah blah here to help you
Blah blah blah could go far
Blah blah blah co-operation
Blah blah blah big gold star
Blah blah blah best behaviour
Blah blah blah quick quick quick
Blah blah blah pull your socks up
Blah blah blah the big stick!
Any questions?
Schoolkids No, Miss.
Kid (*raising a hand*) I d-d-don't understand.
Teacher A troublemaker. Playtime!
Schoolkids Yeah!

Schoolkids get up and start to play. They approach and encircle Kid, jeering and poking

Schoolkid 1 You're fat.
Schoolkid 2 You're a gimp.
Schoolkid 3 You look like a chimp.
Schoolkid 4 You stutter when you talk.
Schoolkid 5 And you limp when you walk.

Schoolkids (*chanting*) You're fat, you're a gimp
You look like a chimp
You stutter when you talk
And you limp when you walk

Schoolkids move off to one side in a playground huddle leaving Kid alone and dejected

Voice At last, something I can relate to. Believe it or not, I too was a lonely child.

Id puts a clown's mask on Kid. Schoolkids return chanting: "You're fat" etc. Kid turns to face them. Seeing the clown's mask they stop chanting. Kid performs a basic magic trick. Schoolkids laugh and crowd around patting Kid on the back

Make 'em laugh, eh? Is that your big message?

New Kid enters

Kid points at New Kid and begins the chant: "You're fat" etc. Schoolkids join in and led by Kid they crowd around New Kid and put the boot in

Really! This needless infant violence is grotesque. Whatever next?

A funereal drum beat

Death, a hooded figure carrying a scythe, enters

Oh Lord! Are we supposed to be taking this seriously?
Id If it please you gentles this figure with black robe and scythe doth represent Death!
Voice Mmm, a tad Bergmanesque, *n'est pas*?

Schoolkids approach Death seemingly unafraid

Id The stranger walks amongst us even in the midst of life.
Schoolkid 1 We greet him as we greet any stranger.
Schoolkid 2 We are shy.
Schoolkid 3 We are curious.
Schoolkid 4 We are trusting.

Drum beat stops. Death waves the scythe over their heads

Schoolkid 5 (*dropping dead*) Leukaemia!
Schoolkid 6 (*dropping dead*) Meningitis!
Kid (*dropping dead*) In-in-in-fanticide!

Crash on drums

Black-out

   Death exits

Chorus return to starting positions

Voice Well, this is cheery, isn't it? I suppose it's meant to be black comedy. There's nothing funny about children dying, you know. Whatever happened to the well-made play, eh?

The Lights come up

Id (*clearing his throat*) Ladies and gentlemen...
Voice Oh God!

Chorus become angst-ridden teenagers. They mill around, some nervously, others strutting aggressively

Id When we become "young adults", we begin to question what is right and what is wrong. What is...
Teen 1 Good and evil.
Teen 2 Black and white.
Teen 3 Truth and lies.

Teen 4 Love and hate.
Id Heaven and... Heaven and... (*He stares vacantly at the audience*)
Voice Oh, I see. It's one of these repetitive cycles. Lull the audience into a false sense of security. Build them up to let them down. Well, I for one am not falling for it. Complete your own sentence.

Id remains frozen. A long silence

No, I'm sorry. As far as I'm concerned you can stand there until it freezes over in hell.
Id Exactly!
Voice Damn!
Id Ladies and gentlemen, there is a certain sublime comfort to be had from challenging these Universal Truths.
Voice Ah! Universal Truths again. Yes, I see a pattern emerging here.

Chorus form a human pyramid. Yoof looks on

Id Without hesitation we begin to question our elders, our parents and teachers, our government, our TV personalities, assured in the belief that they live their lives by a corrupt code of moral conduct of which we try to purge ourselves on a daily basis. Friends, do you remember your surprise when...?

A drum roll

Voice Yes, here we go again.

Yoof climbs the human pyramid. This time it stands firm. Chorus sound a vaudevillian fanfare: "Ta-da!"

At last! A dramatic turning point. The triumph of the human spirit perhaps?
Yoof You're tearing me apart!

The pyramid begins to waver then collapses accompanied by a crash on the drums

Voice What was that, then? "Rebel Without Applause"? I suppose you imagine that a couple of pop culture references will lend your piece some spurious post-modern street credibility. Well, think again.
Id Ladies and gentlemen, it is a well documented "fact" that most of our youth is spent in a constant state of...
Teen 1 Confusion!
Teen 2 Anxiety!
Teen 3 Alienation!
Id Spent in a fruitless search for...
Teen 4 Approval!
Teen 5 Unconditional love!
Teen 6 Gratification!
Id To summarise, then...
Teenagers I hate my Mummy!
Id Ladies and gentlemen, an illustration.

Heavy traffic effect. In a pool of Light C, *Mum, Dad and Yoof mime travelling in a car*

Yoof I am seventeen years old. This is my old lady. And this is my old man. I wish he'd crash this car. I wish they'd burn and die horribly. I wish... I wish...

The car stops and they alight

Mum Time to wipe off that silly smirk!
Dad Time you earned your keep, young Turk!
Id Time for work! (*He rings a bell*)

Office

Chorus become Workers and crowd around Boss dutifully

Boss Gather round, guys. Today we have someone new joining the organisation.
Workers OK!

Secretary ushers Yoof to Boss

Boss Say "Hi" to the team.

With beaming smiles, Workers queue up to shake Yoof's hand. As they file past their smiles turn to grimaces and they mime stabbing Yoof in the back

Worker 1 Welcome on board!
Worker 2 We're all one big happy family.
Worker 3 My door's always open.
Worker 4 Don't be a stranger!
Worker 5 You don't have to be mad to work here...
Boss But it helps!

Workers laugh sycophantically

Now pay attention, guys.

Boss snaps his fingers and Secretary reads from dictation notes

Secretary   Blah blah blah here to help you
                      Blah blah blah could go far
                      Blah blah blah co-operation
                      Blah blah blah company car
                      Blah blah blah monthly targets
                      Blah blah blah scratch my back
                      Blah blah blah pull your weight
                      Blah blah blah...
Boss The sack! Any questions?
Workers No, Sir!
Yoof (*raising his hand*) When do we get paid?

Boss A troublemaker.
Worker 1 Time you learned to hold your tongue.
Worker 2 Time you tried to play along.
Id Time for a song.

Song 1: Time is money

Boss
Time is money, money is time
Each day on earth, what is it worth?
That's the bottom line
Time is costly, time ain't cheap
I'll tell you something sonny
Time is money, time is money.

Secretary (*reading notes*) Time is money
Money is time
The seconds tick
The meter clicks
Even in your prime
Each hour is valued
Till your day is done
I'll tell you something honey
Time is money, time is money.

Chorus Time is money
Money is time
Tock
Clock

Five, six, seven
Steps to heaven.

Boss No time to lose...
Secretary No time to schmoose...
Boss No time to lace up your shoes...
Secretary No time to blink...
Boss No time to think...
Secretary ⎫
Boss ⎬ (*together*) No time to sing the blues.
Chorus Time is money, money is time
The seconds tick, the meter clicks
Even in your prime

	Each hour is valued till your day is done
	I'll tell you something funny
	Time is money time is money…
	Time is money time is money…
Boss	Time…
Secretary	Time is money.
Boss	Time…
Secretary	Time is money.
All	Time is money.

Boss (*speaking*) OK, let's go to work!

Computer chatter. Chorus form a chair and computer screen. Yoof sits down and keys in instructions

Yoof Enter.
Computer Error.
Yoof Enter.
Computer Error.
Yoof Damn! Enter, enter…
Computer Error. You're not very good at this, are you?
Yoof There must be more to life than this.
Computer Error.
Boss Payday!

Boss hands out pay packets to Chorus, who crowd around greedily

(*Taking Yoof aside*) Time to think about your future. Time to put a little something aside. Time to…
Workers Live a little!

Mime and dance sequence. Music: heavy drum beat. Chorus become Clubbers. Dividing into two camps, Female and Male, they take to either side of the stage. Females put on brassieres over their costumes and Males put on Y-front underpants over their costumes. Yoof watches all this with some confusion. He goes to join one camp and then the other but is undecided. Finally Yoof puts on a bra and a pair of underpants and stands apart from either camp

Nightclub

The Lights flash in time to the drum beat. With synchronised movement both camps make as if drinking heavily and eyeing up the opposite camp. Making for the toilets both camps cross the dance floor. As they pass, they sniff around each other like dogs and bitches. Yoof looks on with some confusion

In the Gents toilet, Males stand in a line as if at urinals. Simultaneously, in the Ladies toilet, Females stand in a line as if at a mirror applying make-up, fixing their hair and adjusting their bras. Both camps make lewd gestures about the opposite camp. Leaving the toilets, Males and Females meet and couple up. Filing past Dealer, they hand over their pay packets and Dealer dispenses them pills from a large jar. Swallowing the pills Clubbers move to the dance floor and dance ecstatically

Yoof wanders about the dance floor left out of the action. He notices Passion who also wears a bra and Y-fronts. They approach each other tentatively, then embrace and dance slowly. Music fades to silence. As it does so, Clubbers slow to a freeze

In a pool of light C, Yoof and Passion remove their bras and pants. Falling to the floor, they begin to make love. As they do so, they roll over so as one becomes passive and the other active and so on. As they climax, they freeze

Id (*with a French accent*) We make love to make life. We live life to make love.
Yoof Now it all makes some sort of sense. I wish... I wish this moment...

A funereal drum beat

   Death enters

Clubbers act cool

Id The stranger walks among us even in the midst of life.
Voice Oh, go away.
Clubber 1 We greet him as we greet any stranger.
Clubber 2 We dance with him.
Clubber 3 We flirt with him.
Clubber 4 We laugh in his face.

The drum beat stops. Death waves the scythe over Yoof and Passion's heads

Yoof Give me an H!

Chorus become Cheerleaders

Cheerleaders H!
Yoof Give me an I!
Cheerleaders I!
Yoof Give me a V!
Cheerleaders V!
Yoof What does it spell?
Cheerleaders The end!
Yoof Are you positive?
Cheerleaders No, but you are!

Yoof and Passion drop dead

Black-out on a drum crash

Death exits

Chorus return to starting positions

Voice If you ask me, this is just a pretentious Pot Noodle of pseudo-philosophical party pieces. Oh, I say, that's rather good. Yes, I can use that.

The Lights come up. Id clears his throat as if to speak

Ladies and gentlemen.

Chorus become middle-aged Muddlers and mill around neurotically

Id When we become "middle-aged" we begin to dictate what is right and what is wrong. What is...
Muddler 1 Good and evil.
Muddler 2 Black and white.
Muddler 3 Truth and lies.
Muddler 4 Love and hate.
Id Heaven and...
Voice Hell. Get on with it.
Id Ladies and gentlemen, there is a certain sublime comfort to be had from dictating these Universal Truths.
Voice Huh! Haven't heard one yet.

Chorus form a human pyramid. Middle Age looks on

Id Without hesitation we begin to disapprove of our peers, our children, their teachers, our government, our TV personalities, assured in the belief that they live their lives by a misguided code of moral conduct from which we try to discourage them on a daily basis. Ladies and gentlemen, it may surprise you when...?

A drum roll

Voice This is so, so predictable.
Middle Age climbs the human pyramid. Again, the crowning triumph is achieved, accompanied by a vaudevillian fanfare from Chorus: "Ta-da!"
Middle Age I made it. Top of the heap!
Voice So what are you telling us—life begins at forty?
Middle Age But is this what I really want?

The pyramid wavers and collapses

Voice We didn't know that was going to happen, did we?

Id Ladies and gentlemen, it is a well documented "fact" that most of our middle age is spent in a constant state of...
Muddler 1 Confusion!
Muddler 2 Anxiety!
Muddler 3 Alienation!
Id Spent in a fruitless search for...
Muddler 4 Approval!
Muddler 5 Unconditional love!
Muddler 6 Gratification!
Id To summarise, then...

Muddlers each turn to a partner and embrace

Muddlers I want you to be my Mummy!
Id Ladies and gentlemen, an illustration.

Motor car effect, tyres squealing. In a pool of light c, Middle Age mimes driving fast and recklessly

Middle Age (*crying*) I was seven years old. I was with my mother and father and we were going to the seaside. I'd never been to the seaside. It was a long way. A long, long way... (*He takes his hands off the steering wheel and closes his eyes*)

Car crash effect. Middle Age slumps over the steering wheel. Two Men-In-White-Coats drag Middle Age from the wreckage

White Coat 1 Time all this stuff was history.
White Coat 2 Time to quit this "me me me".
Id Time for therapy! (*He rings a bell*)

Psychiatric ward

Chorus become Patients and crowd around Shrink anxiously

Shrink Gather round, people. Today we have someone new joining the session.

Patients (*moaning*) Awww...

Men-In-White-Coats usher Middle Age into the group

Shrink Why don't you share with the group and tell us what's wrong with you?
Middle Age Well I... I don't know.

Patients cast their eyes to heaven and make "ga-ga" signs

Shrink Lunatic! Now pay attention, people.
Blah blah blah—here to help you
Blah blah blah—meaningful role
Blah blah blah—co-operation
Blah blah blah—personal gaol
Blah blah blah—tough but tender
Blah blah blah—mental block
Blah blah blah—pull yourself together
Blah blah blah—electric shock
Any questions?

Patients bombard Shrink with questions and fight with each for attention. Shrink raises a hand and they stop, then approaches Middle Age who has remained silent

What about you?
Middle Age What about me?
Shrink Good question. (*He thinks hard for a moment*) Pill time!

Patients file past Shrink who dispenses pills to them from a large jar

(*Rhythmically*) Valium, Mogadon, Librium, Prozac...
Patients Valium, Mogadon, Librium, Prozac...

Patients each receive a pill but there is one pill too many. Shrink shrugs and swallows it. Chorus swallow their pills too and immediately become pacified, milling around in a daze

Song 2: The Depression Song
   (*Singing*) Pills and powders, pacifiers
   Tiny, tempting tranquillisers
   Any old anaesthetizers
   Give them all to me...
Shrink (*to Middle Age*) Now let me guess
   Your life is in a mess
   You're suffering from stress
   Didn't bother to get dressed
   Or brush your hair this morning
   Yes? Yes, it's time to confess
   Why not get it off your chest
   You're depressed.

   You thought you had it made
   Thought you'd made the grade
   When life handed you a lemon
   You made a lemonade
   And now each day you find
   Your life is in a grind
   The things you do are driving you
   Out of your tiny mind.

(*Speaking*) Go on, admit it.

Chorus forms a line and pick Middle Age up as if he were reclining in a psychiatric couch

Chorus   You're depressed...
Middle Age (*speaking*) No.
Chorus   Your life is in a mess...
Middle Age I'm not really at my best.
Chorus   You're suffering from stress...
Middle Age God I need a rest.
Chorus   Didn't bother to get dressed
                    Or brush your hair this morning
                    Yes?

Middle Age Yes.
Chorus Yes, it's time to confess?
Middle Age Yes, I confess.
Chorus Why not get it off your chest?
Middle Age Yes.
Chorus You're depressed.
Middle Age Yes, I'm depressed.
Chorus Ha, ha, ha, ha, ha, ha, ha...
Middle Age So depressed.
Chorus Ha, ha, ha, ha, ha, ha, ha...
Middle Age Ohh.
Chorus Ha, ha, ha, ha, ha, ha, ha...
Middle Age I'm depressed.
Shrink So, why don't we begin at the beginning?
Middle Age I don't know. Why don't we?
Shrink Why don't we what?
Middle Age Why don't we begin at the beginning?
Shrink No, no, you misunderstand me. Why don't we start at the beginning?
Middle Age I thought we did. God!
Shrink OK then, why don't we start at the end?

Chorus search in confusion for the "end"

Middle Age Start at the end? I don't know! I don't know! All these questions!
Shrink I mean why don't we work backwards?
Middle Age I can't imagine. Why don't we work backwards? Yes, that's where I've been going wrong!

Chorus begin to literally work backwards, mechanically doing everything in reverse

Shrink No, no, no. Look, why don't you tell me the first thing that comes into your head?

Confusion of thought: some of Chorus begin to make love with each other, some attack each other, whilst others hang themselves

Middle Age Really, I couldn't.
Shrink Come, come, just say the first thing that comes into your head.
Middle Age The first thing that comes into your head.
Shrink No, don't say "the first thing that comes into your head". Tell me the first thing that comes into your head.
Middle Age But what if the first thing that comes into my head is the first thing that comes into my head?
Shrink Very well. (*He pauses*) I hear you have a new movie coming out.
Middle Age Yes. It's called "Screwed Up"!
Shrink Perhaps the folks would like to hear what it's all about. Mmm?

Chorus applaud like a TV studio audience

Middle Age Well, it revolves around a group of forty-something intellectuals, slash, artists, each going through a mid-life crisis and their search for self-knowledge, slash, personal fulfilment, through a series of meaningless, slash, meaningful, affairs with their best friend's partner, slash, children, slash, therapist, slash... Wrists.
Shrink I think we have a clip. Yes, here it is.

Music: tinkly jazz piano. Cocktail party

Chorus become sophisticated Party-Goers, standing around chatting

Party-Goer 1 God, I'm so depressed.
Party-Goer 2 You're depressed? What have you got to be depressed about? A fulfilling career, a fabulous penthouse apartment, a beautiful teenage mistress, your health... You've got nothing to be depressed about.
Party-Goer 1 I know, I know, that's what's so depressing.

Party-goers laugh. A funereal drum beat

Death enters and walks amongst the Party-Goers

They are frightened

Voice Not again!
Id *This* is a recurring motif.
Voice Ooo, a recurring motif!
Id The stranger walks amongst us even in the midst of life.
Party-Goer 1 We greet him as we greet any stranger.
Party-Goer 2 With fear.
Party-Goer 3 With loathing.
Party-Goer 4 With anger.

The drum beat stops. Death waves the scythe over Party-Goers' heads

Party-Goer 1 (*dropping dead*) Heart attack!
Party-Goer 2 (*dropping dead*) Cirrhosis of the liver!
Middle Age C-ca-can-canc...
Voice Don't say it!

Middle Age drops dead. Black-out on a drum crash

Death exits

Chorus return to starting positions

Is nothing sacred? What I'd like to know is whether there's a point to any of this. I think not.

The Lights come up

Id (*clearing his throat*) Ladies and gentlemen, when we become...

Chorus shuffle around like geriatrics

Voice Let me guess—"Senior Citizens"?
Id When we become "Old Farts", we begin to forget what is right and what is...
Voice Wrong ... good and evil ... black and white ... heaven and

hell. Now for God's sake hurry up and make your point. I have an *après*-theatre supper to get to.

Id Ladies and gentlemen, there is a certain sublime comfort to be had from disregarding these Universal Truths.

Voice And another thing, I've paid good money to see this so-called entertainment. When are we going to get one of these Universal Truths you keep talking about, eh?

Chorus form a human pyramid but they are old and frail and it is done slowly with great difficulty. Old Fart looks on

Id With nostalgia we remember our elders, our parents and teachers, our government, our TV personalities, assured in the belief that they, too, lived their lives by the same incontrovertible code of moral conduct that they bullied into us on a daily basis.

A drum roll. Old Fart approaches the human pyramid, goes to climb it, then hesitates

Old Fart Forget it!

The pyramid collapses

Id Ladies and gentlemen, it is a well documented "fact" that most of our old age is spent in a constant state of...
Geriatric 1 Confusion!
Geriatric 2 Anxiety!
Geriatric 3 Alienation!
Id Spent in a fruitless search for...
Geriatric 4 Approval!
Geriatric 5 Unconditional love!
Geriatric 6 Gratification!
Id To summarise, then...
Geriatrics I want my ... nurse!
Id Ladies and gentlemen, an illustration.

Heavy traffic effect. Old Fart, Son and Daughter mime travelling in a car. Son and Daughter in front, Old Fart in the back

Old Fart I am seventy years old. This is my son. And this is my daughter. We are going… Where are we going?

The car stops. Son and Daughter help Old Fart out of the car

Son Time to head on down the hill.
Daughter Time to plant some daffodils.
Id Time to make a will! (*He rings a bell*)

Retirement home

Chorus become Geriatrics and crowd around Nurse dutifully

Nurse (*shouting*) Gather round, folks. Today we have someone new joining the home.
Geriatrics (*straining to hear*) Eh?

Son and Daughter escort a struggling Old Fart to Nurse

Old Fart No, no, no…
Son Yes!
Daughter Yes!
Nurse (*grabbing Old Fart*) Yes! Tell the other clients how old you are.
Old Fart I'm… I'm…
Nurse   Stupid old fart! Now pay attention, folks.
              Blah blah blah here to help you
              Blah blah blah have to shout
              Blah blah blah co-operation
              Blah blah blah big day out
              Blah blah blah best behaviour
              Blah blah blah nice and neat
              Blah blah blah don't pull your bell
              Blah blah blah rubber sheet!
              No time for questions. It's exercise time!

Chorus shuffle around in a circle

Geriatric 1	Time was when I was younger
	When time didn't matter...
Geriatric 2	Time was longer when I was younger
	I was free of time...
Geriatric 3	Free time was all I had
	Time to be me when I was a youngster...
Geriatric 4	Every day lasted longer
	It lasted longer because it didn't matter...
Geriatric 1	For that matter I didn't think how quick it passed...
Geriatric 2	How long it would last...
Geriatric 3	Days were endless...
Geriatric 4	Nights the same...
Geriatric 1	Filled with dreams of endless days...
Geriatric 2	Days, nights, it didn't matter...
Geriatric 3	It didn't matter because it had no meaning...
Geriatric 4	Only dreaming when I was younger...
Old Fart	There was a particular day
	A day in particular I remember
	I remember that day like yesterday
	It stretched to...
Geriatrics	Infinity.

Motor car effect. Mum, Dad, and Kid mime travelling in a car. The mood this time is different; a warm, nostalgic glow surrounding everything. Old Fart and Geriatrics look on

Old Fart	We went to the seaside
	The car journey took forever
	I said...
Kid	Mummy, aren't we there yet?
	We must be there.
Mum (*soothingly*)	No.
Old Fart	She said...
Mum	A little longer, a little further.
Old Fart	It took forever...

Seaside. Seaside sounds

The Family get out of the car and spread themselves on the beach. Dad smokes a pipe, Mum knits. Kid looks out to the sea and sky with wide-eyed wonder

	When we got there I lay on the beach and stared at the sky
	The wide, blue yonder
	I said...
Kid	Mummy? Who made the sky?
Mum	My!
Old Fart	She said...
Mum	God made the sky
	Be good and you'll fly way up there when you die.
Old Fart	I swam in the sea
	Wide and bottomless it stretched to...
Geriatrics	Infinity.
Old Fart	The sea, the sky, the day
	Endless
	I said...
Kid	Daddy, why can't we live forever?
Dad	Why?
Old Fart	He said...
Dad	I don't know why
	Now, be good and eat your pie.

Traffic effect. Family mime travelling in a car

Old Fart	When we drove home it took forever
	I thought we'd never get home
	Ever
	I said...
Kid	Mummy, aren't we home yet?
	We must be soon.
Mum	No.

Old Fart	She said…
Mum	A little further, a little longer.
Old Fart	It took forever
	But it didn't matter
	It didn't matter when I was younger
	Nothing mattered but the moment
	Each moment mattered more than any moment before
	Nothing mattered but Now
	But now…

A funereal drum beat

Death enters

Geriatrics greet him with open arms

Voice Well, look who's here!
Id The stranger walks amongst us even in the midst of life.
Geriatric 1 We greet him as we greet any old friend.
Geriatric 2 We welcome him.
Geriatric 3 We embrace him.
Geriatric 4 We walk with him.

Death waves the scythe over Old Fart and Geriatrics' heads. They wither and drop dead. The Lights dim to create a bleak atmosphere. Death approaches the audience. The drum stops beating

Id Time is up!

Death waves the scythe over the audience. Silence, a chilling moment. Id approaches and pulls off Death's hood to reveal that he is wearing a clown's mask. Chorus come back from the dead. They laugh hysterically and point at the audience mockingly

Voice All right, stop this! I've seen enough. Quiet!

Chorus hang their heads like naughty children caught in the act

What do you think you're doing? If you ask me this is nothing more than the self-indulgent ramblings of a sick and demented mind. Life reduced to a cruel, meaningless joke. What ever happened to pure escapism? Good old-fashioned show business?
Id *This* is Art!
Chorus (*defiantly*) Yeah!
Voice Art, eh? Well, I don't know about Art, but I do know what I don't like and I want my money back!

Chorus look at Id aghast. The game is up

Id (*clearing his throat*) Ladies and gentlemen, we present good, old-fashioned show business!

        Song 3: Blah, Blah, Blah
        (*Singing*) Like it or not we're in the human race
        And from the crib until our six-foot space
        There is one fact we might as well all face
        This world can be a funny old place...

Chorus   Blah, blah, blah, blah, blah, blah, blah
        You're born, you live, you die
        You climb, you fall, you cry
        But no-one knows just why
        You're born, you live, you die.

Chorus 1   Is this all a rehearsal
        For a much better play?
        Is there truth universal?
        Who gives a toss anyway?
        Boo, boo, be, doo!

Chorus   Blah, blah, blah, blah, blah, blah, blah
        Blah, blah, blah, blah, blah, blah, blah
        You're born, you live, you die
        You meet, you mate, goodbye
        And here's the biggest lie

	You're born, you live, you die.
Chorus 2	Is there a heaven above us? Are we all on our way To another sad circus? The same old show, different day.
Raspberry effect	
Chorus	Blah, blah, blah, blah, blah, blah, blah Blah, blah, blah, blah, blah, blah, blah You're born (you're born) You live (you live) You die (you die) You hope (you hope) You dream (you dream) You try (you try) But no-one knows just why You're born, you live, you die. You're born, you live, you die.
Id	To make any sense of life's Cruel play The only thing that you can Say is…
Chorus	Blah, blah, blah.

They exit over music reprise

FURNITURE AND PROPERTY LIST

Further dressing may be added at the director's discretion

On stage: Scroll
　　　　　Soapbox
　　　　　Clown's mask
　　　　　Brassieres
　　　　　Y-front underpants
　　　　　Large jar containing pills
　　　　　School bell
　　　　　Magic trick

Off stage: Scythe (**Death**)

Personal: **Death**: hood, clown's mask

LIGHTING PLOT

Property fittings required: nil
Various interior and exterior settings

To open: Fade up lights very slowly to music

Cue 1   Heavy traffic effect is heard (Page 3)
Pool of light on **Mum**, **Dad**, *and* **Kid**

Cue 2   Crash on drums is heard (Page 7)
Black-out

Cue 3   **Voice**: "…to the well-made play, eh?" (Page 7)
Bring up lights

Cue 4   Heavy traffic effect is heard (Page 9)
Pool of light on **Mum**, **Dad**, *and* **Yoof**

Cue 5   **Yoof** stands apart in nightclub scene (Page 12)
Flash lights in time to drum beat

Cue 6   **Clubbers** slow to a freeze (Page 13)
Pool of light on **Yoof** *and* **Passion**

Cue 7   **Yoof** and **Passion** drop dead (Page 14)
Black-out

Cue 8   **Voice**: "Yes, I can use that." (Page 14)
Bring up lights

Cue 9	Squeal of car tyres is heard *Pool of light on* **Middle Age**	(Page 16)
Cue 10	**Middle Age** drops dead *Black-out*	(Page 21)
Cue 11	**Voice**: "I think not." *Bring up lights*	(Page 21)
Cue 12	**Old Fart** and **Geriatrics** drop dead *Dim lights for bleak atmosphere*	(Page 26)

EFFECTS PLOT

Cue 1	To open *Long, ominous drone of opening chord of Pink Floyd's* Shine On You Crazy Diamond; *smoke effect*	(Page 1)
Cue 2	**Chorus 1** knees **Id** in the crotch *Crash on drums*	(Page 1)
Cue 3	**Id**: "…remember your surprise when…" *Drum roll*	(Page 3)
Cue 4	The human pyramid collapses *Crash on drums*	(Page 3)
Cue 5	**Id**: "Ladies and gentlemen, an illustration." *Heavy traffic effect*	(Page 3)
Cue 6	**Mum** and **Dad**: "Shut up!" *Effect of waves crashing and holiday makers making merry*	(Page 4)
Cue 7	**Voice**: "Whatever next?" *Funereal drum beat*	(Page 6)
Cue 8	**Schoolkid 4**: "We are trusting." *Cut drum beat*	(Page 7)
Cue 9	**Kid**: "In-in-in-fanticide!" *Crash on drums*	(Page 7)

Cue 10	**Id**: "…remember your surprise when…?" *Drum roll*	(Page 8)
Cue 11	The human pyramid collapses *Crash on drums*	(Page 9)
Cue 12	**Id**: "Ladies and gentlemen, an illustration." *Heavy traffic effect*	(Page 9)
Cue 13	**Workers**: "Live a little." *Music: heavy drum beat*	(Page 12)
Cue 14	**Yoof** and **Passion** dance slowly *Fade music*	(Page 13)
Cue 15	**Yoof**: "I wish this moment…" *Funereal drum beat*	(Page 13)
Cue 16	**Clubber 4**: "We laugh in his face." *Cut drum beat*	(Page 14)
Cue 17	Black-out *Crash on drums*	(Page 14)
Cue 18	**Id**: "…may surprise you when…?" *Drum roll*	(Page 15)
Cue 19	**Id**: "Ladies and gentlemen, an illustration." *Motor car effect, tyres squealing*	(Page 16)
Cue 20	**Middle Age** closes his eyes *Car crash effect*	(Page 16)
Cue 21	**Shrink**: "Yes, here it is." *Music: tinkly jazz piano*	(Page 20)
Cue 22	**Party-Goers** laugh *Funereal drum beat*	(Page 20)

Cue 23	**Party-Goer 4**: "With anger." *Cut drum beat*	(Page 21)
Cue 24	**Middle Age** drops dead *Crash on drums*	(Page 21)
Cue 25	**Id**: "…bullied into us on a daily basis." *Drum roll*	(Page 22)
Cue 26	**Id**: "Ladies and gentlemen, an illustration." *Heavy traffic effect*	(Page 22)
Cue 27	**Geriatrics**: "Infinity." *Motor car effect*	(Page 24)
Cue 28	**Old Fart**: "It took forever…" *Seaside sounds*	(Page 24)
Cue 29	**Dad**: "Now, be good and eat your pie." *Traffic effect*	(Page 25)
Cue 30	**Old Fart**: "But now…" *Funereal drum beat*	(Page 26)
Cue 31	**Death** approaches the audience *Cut drum beat*	(Page 26)
Cue 32	**Chorus 2**: "…old show, different day." *Raspberry effect*	(Page 28)
Cue 33	**Chorus** and **Id** exit *Music reprise*	(Page 28)

www.ingramcontent.com/pod-product-compliance
Ingram Content Group UK Ltd.
Pitfield, Milton Keynes, MK11 3LW, UK
UKHW021848210426
5322IPUK00022B/542

9 780573 152108